FROM THE CREATOR

A network catalog to expand and expose authors, consulting/coaching businesses, content creators, speakers, pastors, ministers; The Professional Wisdom Network (PWN) .

FIRST national book publication dedicated solely to women and men empowerment.

The purpose of this catalog is to help individuals package and present. Making their presence known and marketing their message.

Create Your World offers private book publishing. For the following , ranging from autobiographical, spiritual, children's and self-help for women and men and anthologies.

 - We will host PWN 2nd annual Authors Brunch Conference at the Center of Hope. Honoring Authors, workshops and networking.

Cassandra Lang

FEATURE

Apostle Redrick E. Jones

Apostle Redrick E. Jones is deeply committed to the work of the Lord, and he has a servant's heart. He is a humble man of God who will assure you that God can deliver you from anything! Apostle R.E. Jones is happily married to his lovely wife Prophetess Audrey L. Jones for 28 years, they are the proud parents of six adult children and twenty grandchildren.

Apostle R.E. Jones is a native of Louisiana. He has been preaching and teaching the Word of God for more than 30 years and he's been in pastoral ministry since 1995. Apostle R.E. Jones served as a Minister at Maranatha Fellowship in South Bend, Indiana for three years.

In 2002, Apostle R.E. Jones founded the Outreach Ministries of Christ Worldwide Fellowship of Churches. Apostle R.E. Jones serves as the OMC presiding prelate and he is also the founder of New Creation Praise and Worship Center (NCPWC) International. NCPWC has locations in Indiana, Louisiana, and Texas.

Apostle R.E. Jones' educational background includes a Bachelors in Theology from The Holy Ghost Theological Institute in South Bend, Indiana. His pursuit of learning God's word and proclaiming God's word has afforded him the opportunity to preach and teach, he travels around the country to share God's plan for Apostolic order in the church.

Apostle R.E. Jones is a man who loves God, God's people, and His Word. He is anointed to rightly divide the Word of Truth with power and conviction while providing tools for practical application that will allow the hearers of the Word to be infinitely transformed. He is known for his dynamic revelatory style of preaching which helps people apply biblical principles to their everyday lives.

Apostle R.E. Jones' distinctive ministry advocates to reach those who may otherwise be left behind, endeavoring to reach the masses through the power of God's agape love. He is a humble, and gifted servant of God whose ultimate desire is to do the will of God.

Paul shares in Romans 8:28 - And we know that all things work together for good to those who love God, to those who are the called according to His purpose. This biblical promise is one of Apostle R.E. Jones' favorite passages of scripture. Loving God and experiencing His call are one, Apostle R.E. Jones is an effective leader who exemplifies both.

Create Your World
WISDOM NETWORK
Empowering Men & Women Worldwide

"You've got a Story, a Voice, and a Message burning inside of you; I'm here to help you release it!"

I'M OFFERING
- Mentorship
- Speech Coaching
(I will help you evolve from being speaking-challenged Novices, into becoming speaking Powerhouses)

CRAFT YOUR MESSAGE: Learn the secrets to structuring speeches that resonate, using your unique experiences.

Cassandra M. Lang
CEO/FOUNDER: WISDOM NETWORK

Cassandra Lang stands as a dynamic force in the world of motivational speaking. With a magnetic presence that captivates audiences, she empowers individuals and groups from diverse backgrounds—whether they are ambitious entrepreneurs, small business owners, or leaders in non-profit organizations and communities. Cassandra's message is simple yet profound: "Use What's In Your House of Value." She encourages everyone to harness their unique talents, package them, and present them to the world.

As an accomplished author of several transformative books, including Create Your World, Discover Yourself, I am A Queen, and Uncover Her Innocent Eyes, Cassandra has inspired countless people to discover their inner strength and potential. Her success tips—ranging from writing the vision to connecting with like-minded individuals—provide a roadmap to achieving greatness.

Cassandra's teachings are deeply rooted in faith and the belief that one's strength is determined by their source. She challenges her audience to identify their source of inspiration, revelation, and transformation, drawing from her own spiritual insights and the wisdom of leaders like Pastor Mike, Jr. Her mantra, inspired by 2 Timothy 1:7, reinforces the belief that we are all endowed with power, love, and self-discipline—tools essential for overcoming the challenges of fear, anger, immaturity, tiredness, and hurt.

With her words, Cassandra Lang doesn't just motivate—she transforms lives, guiding others to realize their full potential and make their unique mark on the world.

You will learn the following in "Write My Story Workshop"
- Your voice anchored in Purpose
- Unleash your Greatness
- Master your Story
- Learn Storytelling

* If you want to learn how to use books and speaking to monetize your message and grow your business, THIS CHALLENGE WILL SHOW YOU HOW! Join the FREE challenge: "Write My Story Workshop"

Call or Email to find out more:
(225) 515-1564
Createyourworld2021@gmail.com

Dr. Ava Brewster-Turner

Dr. Ava Brewster-Turner is a native Arkansan and resident of Baton Rouge, LA. She dedicated 45 years to education across the states of Arkansas, Tennessee, Illinois, Texas and Louisiana.

Dr. Brewster-Turner's appointments in academia include Assistant to Dean of Liberal Arts at Baton Rouge Community College; Associate Dean and Director of Theatre at Wiley College (Marshall, TX); and Associate Tenured Professor at Southern University(Baton Rouge, LA), just to name a few.

In 2002, Dr. Brewster-Turner founded UpStage Theatre Company due to the absence of Black theatre in Baton Rouge. UpStage Theatre is a 21st century testament to W.E.B. DuBois' manifesto: "We must have a theatre by us, for us and about us". As Founding Artistic Director, she enriched the city of Baton Rouge and surrounding areas with an award-winning community theatre which attracts diverse audiences.

Dr. Brewster-Turner is a true leader who understands the dynamics of following having served as President of the National Association of Dramatic and Speech Arts and State Liaison for the American Association of Community Theatre. Among her other laudable accomplishments are: Recognized by the Baton Rouge Metropolitan City Council for her twenty- years of leadership at UpStage Theatre, 2023 Recipient of the Director's Arts Award from Extensions of Excellence Performing Arts of Shreveport, Appointed to the Creative Arts Team for the historic Baton Rouge Lincoln Theater, Inducted into the Augusta, Arkansas Hall of Fame, Recipient of the 2016 Southern Black Theatre Festival Regional Trailblazer Award, Outstanding Director's Award at Louisiana PlayFest of the American Association of Community Theatre, Directed the Louisiana Black Hall of Fame Tribute honoring Baton Rouge native, Lynn Whitfield, Directed a collaborative tribute production between UpStage Theatre and Southwest College in Los Angeles for the late Ruby Dee.

Dr. Brewster-Turner received a Bachelor of Science in Speech and Theatre from Grambling State University, a M.Ed. Mass Communication/Educational Media from Southern University and Ph.D. in Theatre from Louisiana State University. She is a Life member of Delta Sigma Theta Sorority, Inc., American Association of Community Theatre, Life member of Grambling University National Alumni Association and Phi Delta Kappa. She is married to Lloyd Turner and they have one son, Terrance.

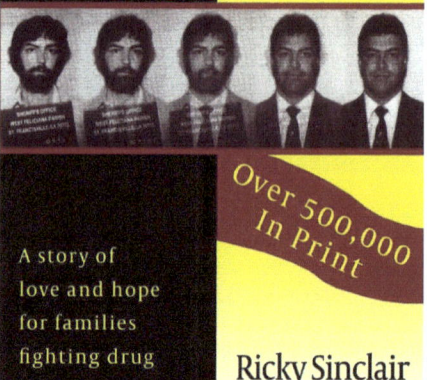

Pastor Ricky Sinclair

Baptism
Sept 29th
11:00 am

Men's Meeting
Second Tuesday of every month
6:30pm

Women's Meeting
Third Saturday of every month
10:30 am

Heaven's Gates & Hell's Flames
October 27 – 29

Kingdom Forward Conference
September 12 – 15

Miracleplacechurch.org

Carlette Garrett

The Story of My Life

I am a 49-year-old single mother of 4 beautiful children, 2 girls, and 2 boys. I was born in New Orleans Charity Hospital by my now-deceased mom, Geraldine Houston.

Upon giving birth to me, my mother became crippled due to an epidural complication. She was unable to raise me by herself, so my Dad, who is now deceased, Albert Harry Porea's mother, and my grandmother, Mary Alice Hill, who is now deceased, took me and raised me from a baby until adulthood.

I grew up in Zachary La. Until I was old enough to be on my own. I was always a church girl. My grandparents kept me in church. I served on the praise team, and the usher board, and I continued serving the Lord throughout my life.
ot my first job working at McDonald's and I got my first apartment when I was 20 years old. I have mainly worked in fast food and retail. I later on became a mother and began to start working towards my goals. One of those goals was to open my own business and I did so and started my own clothes line. It wasn't as successful as I had planned but I hope to get it back up and running soon.

When I reached the age of 40, my kidneys started giving me problems and I later found out I needed dialysis. So, I have been undergoing treatment since then. I was ordained as a Pastor in 2021 under the leadership of Apostle Aihkem Wilson of Christ Embassy International Ministries.

I plan to someday as the Lord leads me to open my own church so that I can be a blessing to many. My heart has always been to see others happy and helping them in whatever way possible. I plan to in the future to do lots of traveling around the world to Minister the Gospel. I am believing God for complete and total healing so that I will be able to fulfill that desire.

My biggest dreams are to eventually get married, become a home owner and open up another business. I am currently a homemaker. This is the story of my life.

Ambassador Coach Ashley Blanshaw

Ambassador Coach Ashley Blanshaw is originally from Brooklyn, NY USA. She is known as the person with many hats. She is a Singer, Songwriter, Music Producer, Solo Music Artist, Motivational Speaker, Business Coach, Ambassador, Global and International Influencer, Activist and Author, and Talk Show Radio Show Host. Her singing and solo music career started at the age of 4 or 5 years old, her Songwriting career started during her freshman year of high school, and her music career started during her college years.

Coach Ashley is also an international bestselling author 20X and writer of 30 books. She has a talk show and radio show: "Worship Experience" with Coach Ashley Blanshaw and "Inspirational Time" with Ashley Blanshaw. She is an activist and advocate for mental health awareness. Coach Ashley is also in the process of becoming a mentor to people who struggle with mental health illness.

Coach Ashley is the founder of the #LoveYurself Campaign for mental health illness. She became certified as a business coach in December 2021. What gives her strength is that her spiritual connection with God, her faith in God and her music connection. Going through this mental illness battle for 24 years, she had struggled with self-confidence and depression as more negativity things, but she realized that she must encourage herself that She is beautiful, strong, empowered, more than a conqueror, a champion, a winner, overcomer, survivor!!!!! She works hard for what she does, and She is also very passionate about in what she does.

Ambassador Coach Ashley is also active in her business, her music, her books and her activism for mental health awareness. Coach Ashley is very active in going into her community to continue to spread and to talk about mental health awareness. Ambassador Coach Ashley is the visionary and host of her ministry: The Chain Breaking Experience event and book anthology and magazine!!!! Her ministry is The Chain Breaking Experience!!!!!! Her ministry encourages the people that the chain has been broken, and Her ministry continues to inspire and encourage people that they are determined to overcome any obstacles and struggles that they are going through, and God is going to make a way for them!!!!!!

She is also a businesswoman with her business: The I am Determined Tour is a community-based business; she travels to the community, hosting and participating in events to continue to spread the importance of mental health awareness. Her business is in New York, but her goal is to continue to expand her business in other states, in the USA, and then in other countries too. She has been doing singing and speaking engagements, virtual and in-person events for the US and other countries like conferences, summits, and mental health rallies. She has hosted a concert for mental health awareness month, and more!!! She also did interviews on talk shows, podcasts, and radio shows too as well.

Her business inspires and encourage people that they are determined to overcome any obstacles and struggles that they going through and God is going to make a way for them!!!!!! Her music is on digital music platforms: Apple Music, Spotify, YouTube and more. Her books are on Amazon and Barnes and Noble.

Contact info and social media:
914-420-2571
ashleyblanshaw@yahoo.com
Facebook: Ambassador Ashley Blanshaw
Facebook Business Page: Coach Ashley Katisha Blanshaw
Facebook Ministry page: The Chain Breaking Experience Event
Instagram: @ambassadorcoachashleyblanshaw2 and @iamdeterminedtour and @thechainbreakingexperience
Twitter: @iamMsAshley
TikTok: @ashleyblanshaw5
LinkedIn and YouTube: Ashley Blanshaw
Clubhouse: @ashleylove595

Annette Chambliss

Annette Chambliss is a Mother of 2 and a Grandmother of 5. She is a member of New Hope Baptist Church and currently an employee of Baton Rouge City-Parish where she is the Executive Assistant in her department.

Annette was recently awarded the distinguished honor as a "Trailblazer" and is also a "Power Diva" within her empowerment group, Power to Exhale, an organization that empowers, uplifts & celebrate women. She is her "Sister's Keeper". Her Spiritual Gift is that of "Exhortation" which is a gift from God to strongly encourage & inspire. Annette applies this gift whenever & wherever she is needed. She also use this gift through her business of Octavia's Bling as an Independent Consultant with Paparazzi Accessories by providing hope & building positive relationships.

One of her favorite scriptures is Jeremiah 29:11 "For I know the plans I have for you, "declares the LORD, "plans to prosper you and not to harm you, plans to give you hope and a future".

Connect with Annette
Website: https://shop.paparazzipremiere.com/OctaviasBling/shop
Facebook: https://www.facebook.com/share/mPhN4bvM6Bo8XBrT/
Shop: https://octavias-bling.square.site/

Evangelist Paulette Davenport

Evangelist Paulette Davenport resides in Zachary, LA, with her husband of 33 years, Elder/Pastor Isaiah Davenport. They have a blended family of five children, ten grandchildren, and seven great-grandchildren.

Paulette was licensed as an Evangelist and Ordained as an Elder on July 9, 2002, by Bishop Earl Johnson and Pastor Clifton Sanford of Macedonia Full Gospel Church. She served in many ministry capacities, specifically in prayer and intercession, which is her first calling and passion. Paulette attended CPM bible college pursuing a degree in Theology.

A board certified and licensed nurse since 1987, and entrepreneur and business owner since 2007, and in 2019, God graced Paulette to pen her life's story and become an Amazon best-selling author. Paulette was reared in Catholicism, but on September 26, 1977, God revealed himself to her on a disco floor in San Francisco, California. She accepted Christ that same night on her living room floor and joined Emmanuel Open Bible Fellowship under Pastor Ronald Miller. On October 9, 1977, she was water baptized and filled with the Holy Spirit and fire on October 23rd, of the same year. In 1978 she had the privilege to travel overseas as a military spouse and God opened a door of utterance to minister and start a prayer and bible study in her home. She had an opportunity to see unlimited signs, wonders, and miracles performed by the hand of God, as HE spoke from the book of Isaiah 58:6.

She is the visionary of the "Midwives at Midnight" Ministry founded in 2006. She is a published best-selling author of her first book titled " Rejected: Unwanted by Others—Pursued by God, released through Amazon in March of 2019.

Evangelist Davenport believes as the bible says, the gifts and Ministry calling are without repentance, but if she had to choose, she would choose the gift of forgiveness and intense intimacy. She has learned, what you behold you will reflect

DNP Publishing

See your Dream in print!!

Our Goal at DNP Publishing is to see your Dream in Print!! Whether you have a manuscript done and ready to go or need help getting it on paper... we are here to help!!!

FROM FULL PACKAGES TO PARTIAL PACKAGES OUR GOAL IS TO WORK WITH YOU TO HELP YOU GET YOUR STORY OUT THERE TO THE WORLD! WE PUBLISH FROM START TO FINISH!

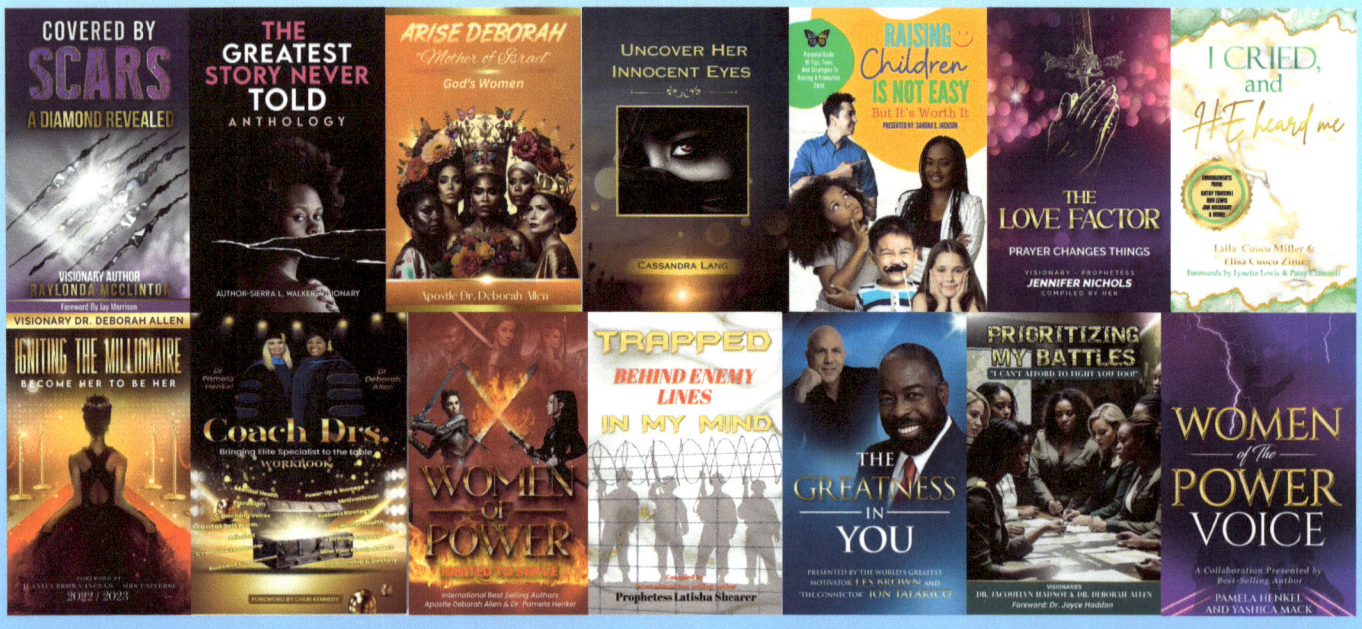

ANTHOLOGY PROJECT MANAGEMENT TO HELP KEEP YOU ON TRACK AND ORGANIZE IT ALL, GRAPHICS FOR LAUNCHES AND BOOK COVER DESIGNS AVAILABLE TO HELP YOU COMPLETE YOUR PROJECTS!
CONNECT WITH US TODAY!!
NICHOL@DNPDESIGNS.COM   WWW.DNPDESIGNS.COM

Evangelist Glenda Ricks

Evangelist Glenda Ricks is a lover of people and has a deep passion for Street Ministry, Children's Ministry, and Prison Ministry. Her love of Children's Ministry led her to start several dance teams and drill teams. She is the head Pastor of Threshold of Faith Outreach Ministry, located in Gonzales, LA. Glenda is a graduate of East Ascension High School and has several Certifications. She attended Word of Life Christian School of Ministry in Darrow, Louisiana, for two years. She also has a certification for Counseling through Christ Center Counseling Center and Leadership Training at New Dimensions Christian Center in Pensacola, Florida. Glenda is the author of "A Glimpse Back To Go Forward" with God.

Glenda's past was preparing me for God's plan for my life. I was the Motor Cycle Queen, the first woman in my area. My friends encouraged me to join their Motorcycle Club. I never thought that would be apart of my life. I later on became a D.J, I spun records for night clubs, it wasn't my desire but I became great at it. All that was training me for ministry. At that time ministry was not on my mind. I said "not me" but God said "yes you ". Life took a big change, I faced a lot of challenges, but God was with me and he brought me through.

John 5:14 states; and this is the confidence that we have in him,that if we ask according to his will he hear us and we know that he hears us. Whatsoever we ask in His name, in the name of Jesus we know we have the petition that we desire of Him. God is so good and I love him so much.

I'm the proud mother of two children Lakeitha and Chaz, and the grandmother of six grandchildren.

Contact info:
P O Box 1161 Gonzales La 70707
225-253-3705

Available to speak at Conferences , Prayer Breakfasts , your next event…

Dr. Latasha Ramsey-Cyprian

Dr. Latasha Ramsey-Cyprian a mother of two, has a successful career in Human Resources. Latasha holds an MBA from LSU-Shreveport reflecting her commitment to continuous learning. She also holds a PhD in Philosophy, acknowledging her dedication to knowledge and contributions in her field. Latasha is also a graduate of Cornell University- Certificate in Women's Entrepreneurship May 2023 and a April 2024 graduate of Milestone Circle Program at Nasdaq Entrepreneurial Center. Latasha works professionally in Human Resources and has 23 years of experience that includes: leadership, staffing employees, payroll, employee benefits and leave management.

Latasha is the owner of Optimum Life Enterprises LLC & Optimum Life Credit Solutions. She is an International Bestselling Author, Credit Repair Specialist, Certified Life Coach, ESL Teacher and International Speaker. Latasha is passionate about providing services that improve the overall quality of life. She focuses heavily on breaking generational curses, women empowerment, and spreading financial literacy.

Latasha started Optimum Life Credit Solutions in June 2020 because she knew that financial literacy equipped us with the knowledge and skill needed to manage money effectively. She is a Board Certified Credit Consultant and Certified Credit Score Consultant. Latasha provides a credit restoration program and business consulting. Latasha hosts seminars in her community that focuses on the process to become a first-time homebuyer and credit restoration. She offers financial planners, basic credit for kids, kids budget planner, business credit, digital budget planner, home buying planner, gratitude journals, Do it Yourself Credit Repair, and surviving debt ebooks.

As a Life Coach, Latasha is dedicated to rewiring an individual's mindset, allowing them to be the very best version of themselves. She's a certified Master Life Coach, certified Happiness Life Coach, certified Goal Success Coach, certified Life Purpose Coach, certified Professional Life Coach, certified Master Mindset Life Coach, certified Confidence Life Coach, certified Emotional Intelligence Life Coach, certified Cognitive Behavioral Life Coach and certified REBT Mindset Life Coach.

Latasha has a signature Life Coaching Program that focuses on accountability, mindset, fear of failure, lack of self-confidence, fear of success, and lack of support. Her coaching program has helped over a hundred clients perform at their fullest potential professionally, personally, and financially.

Latasha is an online ESL Teacher. She teaches students in China English as a second language. She is certified Teaching English to Speakers of Other Languages and certified Teaching English as a Foreign Language. She's able to assist in giving students a leg up in the global job market by providing an emphasis on English language education.

Latasha became an author in 2021, and she is an 8-time best-selling author. She has contributed to 17 anthologies, and she has self-published 5 children's financial literacy books. Latasha loves being an author because it allows her to express her creative side.

Latasha has spoken on several local and international platforms. She enjoys speaking on topics such as women empowerment, educating our youth on finances, and the importance of communities that thrive. She speaks out on global issues because she believes that if people are aware of the issues, they will see the importance of personally taking social action.

Latasha is the Louisiana State Chair of G100 Oneness & Wisdom Wing. She is the board president of Catch My Heart Outreach non-profit organization. She is a member of ForbesBLK, LSUS Alumni Association and a member of National Black MBA Association. She is a member of Gamma Phi Delta Sorority Inc.

Latasha's active involvement in the community makes a difference. She enjoys speaking to children and teenagers about financial literacy so they can build strong money habits early on and avoid many of the mistakes that lead to lifelong money struggles. Latasha has been featured in several magazines and she aims to empower, encourage and inspire through credit education and challenges individuals to have an abundant mindset. Latasha, a 2023 recipient of the Presidential Lifetime Achievement Awards and Global Impact Leadership Award enjoys volunteering and serving her community.

To connect:
Email: info@optimumlifecreditsolutions.com
or visit
https://www.optimumlifecreditsolutions.com/

Dr. Monique Rodgers

Dr. Monique Rodgers is an ordained prophet, visionary, intercessor, international best-selling author, CEO, motivational speaker, entrepreneur, educator, and literary genius. Dr. Rodgers excels today as a notable writing coach, founder, and serial entrepreneur. She is a first year kindergarten teacher at Restoration Community Academy located in Alpharetta, GA. Dr. Monique Rodgers was recently inducted into Kappa Delta Phi which is a distinguished honor community for educators of excellence. She also received an educator of the year award in 2022 from Fire Leadership by Chavon Anette. In 2023 she received The Presidential Lifetime Achievement Award.

Throughout the course of her career, she has written such prolific works such as, Hello! My name is Millennial, Picking up the Pieces, The Majestical Land of Twinville, Falling in Love with Jesus, Accelerate, Overcoming Writer's Block, Speak Reach and Inspire, Just Breathe, I am Black History and Called to Intercede Volumes 1-14 and many more. She has also been included as a co-author in collaborations such as, Jumpstart Your Mind, Speak Up We Deserve to Be Heard, Finding Joy in the Journey Volume 2, and Let the Kingdompreneurs Speak. Due to her outstanding breadth of experience, Dr. Rodgers has been featured on Rachel Speaks radio program, The Love Walk Podcast, The Glory Network, God's Glory Radio Show, The Miracle Zone, The Healing Zone. She also graced several platforms worldwide. She served as a TV host for WATCTV. She has been featured in Heart and Soul Magazine, My Story the Magazine, Kish Magazine's Top 20 National Authors of 2021. Marquis Who's Who in America 2021-2022. She also assisted in various volunteer work including an executive team member for Lady Deliverer's Arise, Aniyah Space and she also a board member for I am my sister organization. She is also a certified master business coach, certified vegan life coach, and health advocate. She has served on various leadership positions in business and in ministry. She is currently a prayer hub leader for the city of Raleigh under the tutelage of Apostle Jennifer LeClaire. She is also a team member of CBK where she serves in ministry for Sofia Ruffin. She is an ambassador for Kingdom Sniper Institute where she serves under the tutelage of Evangelist Latrice and Elder Dereck Ryan. She has also been on staff with Dr. Patricia Bailey as an armor bearer, social media assistant, books and products manager. As an expert in her field Dr. Rodgers earned her undergraduate degree through Oral Roberts University as well as a Master of Science degree and a doctorate in global leadership through Colorado Technical University. She has also studied at the Black Business School online as well as Harvard University Business Online. Looking towards the future, Dr. Rodgers intends to expand upon her expertise and continue serving through ministry for God. She aspires to help over one hundred authors to complete and publish their books and help intercessors to draw closer to God.

Elissa Boudreaux

https://info077330.wixsite.com/lotusworldwideconsul

Elissa Boudreaux mother of two beautiful young ladies 15-29 years old, a two-time 100% disabled war veteran, serving both in Operations Desert Shield/Storm/Sortee' and Operation Enduring Freedom, I experienced domestic violence for 24 years and has been a survivor for 15 years, I established a non-profit organization called X-Posed Domestic Violence. Our organization aims to raise awareness and promote social norms that reject domestic violence through education and awareness campaigns.

Through my efforts, I have developed a network of community leaders and connected with residents to educate them on domestic violence education and resources. In addition, I founded Lotus Worldwide Consulting, LLC in 2016 with the objective of providing educational seminars to perpetrators, families, friends, groups, businesses, and organizations on the growing problem of domestic abuse. My ultimate goal is to bring awareness and expose the silent killer to people from all walks of life, all over the world. Through my work, I have seen firsthand the devastating effects that domestic violence can have on families and communities. It is a complex issue that requires a multifaceted approach, which is why we offer a variety of services to meet the diverse needs of those affected by domestic abuse. Our seminars and workshops provide education on the warning signs of domestic violence, how to seek help, and how to support those who have experienced abuse. Our coaching and consulting services offer personalized support to individuals who are experiencing or have experienced abuse or want self-development, helping them to navigate the complex emotions and challenges that come with leaving an abusive situation or navigating life's challenges.

Ultimately, our goal is to create a world where domestic violence is no longer tolerated. We believe that everyone has the right to feel safe and secure in their home, and we will continue to work tirelessly to make that a reality. I think about how life can be so fragile and how quickly it can be taken away. I know firsthand the effect of this silent killer, and I want to help make a difference in any way I can. Whether it's through volunteering, donating to charity, or loving on them and simply spreading awareness, I believe that we all have the power to make a positive impact on the world.

Kathleen Cooke

Kathleen Cooke is an award-winning producer, actor, global speaker, writer, and co-founder of the multi-award-winning media production company Cooke Media Group and the nonprofit The Influence Lab. She is the founder of Influence Women, an initiative of The Influence Lab, with branches in Hollywood and multiple U.S. cities, offering career development and a faith community for women in the film, television, music, and arts industries. She was awarded a National Congressional Leadership Award in 2022 in Washington D.C and is the author of "Hope 4 Today: Stay Connected to God in a Distracted Culture." She has appeared on top national and international radio, podcasts, and television shows, including CBN and TBN, and her articles have been published by Avail Leadership, Charisma, Empowered, and Canvas Rebel Magazines.

"Influence Women" is raising up a confident new generation of female leaders in media, entertainment, arts and leadership.

https://influencewomen.org

Productions

See your Dream in Production!!

Our Goal at DNP Productions is to see your Dream of your own show come to life!! Whether you have a FB live you have been doing or just a concept for a show. We are here to help!!!

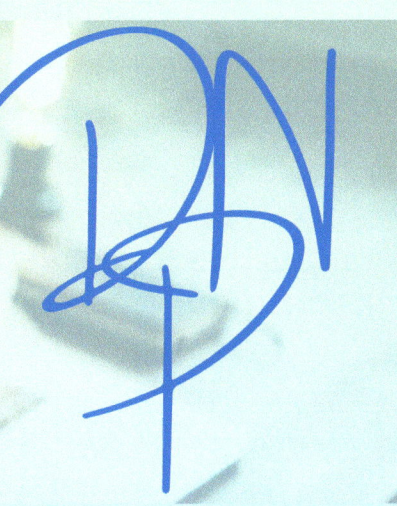

CONTACT US TODAY... NICHOL@DNPDESIGNS.COM   WWW.DNPDESIGNS.COM

Lady Lexx

Alexis is a licensed and ordained Minister, Writer, Public Speaker, Administrator and Inspirational Hip Hop recording Artist. She is a 2011 graduate of BRCC, a 2012 and 2015 graduate of Southern University A&M College, where she received her BS and MS, and she completed her PhD in Urban Planning Natural Resources in 2020.

"Lexx" advocates and supports victims of violent crimes, as well as the children of victims of violent crimes. She takes great pride in being a Mentor, as she seeks to influence the lives of children, youth, men and woman, through God's word and through the testaments of her life's many trials, failures, and accomplishments. She is a community partner in educating and empowering others concerning the environmental impacts of our choices and decisions. In her professional career, she a Disciplinarian at a Baton Rouge Charter that supports children with learning difficulties. She aspires daily to encourage teachers, parents, staff, and students that overcoming any challenge is possible.

As a recording artist, she has touched many lives as she has performed and witnessed Gods greatness. She has also written a book entitled "Mixed Emotions." It is a collection of daily devotionals written throughout the process of her metamorphosis and transformation to Ministry.

Her latest album project is found on music distribution sites, such as, Spotify, iTunes, Tidal, Google Play and YouTube! Singles include "We The Chose" and "Amazing God" and "Street Gospel." Her current single entitled "Faith On Dumb," which is available on all major platforms. She is spreading her ministry through song (Inspirational Hip Hop), social media post and dialogues, touring schools, churches, special events, with the mission of encouraging and informing youth on the benefits of having the right attitudes, striving for success, and unlocking the privileges of God's Kingdom.

https://www.thelexxlifemovement.com/

Shirlette Powell

Creative Entrepreneur Shirlette Powell here!
#ShineOnSis

Welcome to my neighborhood! I am wife to Minister Joseph Powell, III and mother of three precocious chain-breakers.

My story is just this:
The world wanted me dead, I chose to BECOME instead… I'm determined to show God what I can do with what He's put in my hand. The picture in my mind's eye is a flat, sandy place littered with jewels. Every precious stone you can think of with shards of broken glass littered throughout. I can see myself standing over this "buried treasure," wondering how to pull out the prize without incurring any pain. I couldn't sidestep my destiny. I'd have to tunnel through it. I've had to walk through the wounds to become the warrior.

Now, you can't tell me what God can't do! This is my coming out season! This is my fight back from the fear. If I can share a piece of myself that will help bring peace to you, I am more than willing. You are a kingdom being built. DIG IT UP!!! We walk. We war. We WIN! Beautiful while in service to Our Father.

Get on up, Queen. Ask Him your questions, He will show you how to become the answer. It's time to shine, Sis. I am Shirlette Powell. Motivational Speaker. Author of Amazon's Bestseller, You Are A Creator! Host of #ShineOnSis! Content Creator and Former Radio Host, Collaborator, and Friend.

Thanks for taking this ride! Check me out on YouTube. I'm @shirlettepowell on Facebook and @_shineonsis on TikTok. Just here sharing my story to see YOU SHINE! I can see myself in you. Let's go.

Shirlette Powell, Author, Wife, Mother, Intercessor Amazon Best Selling Author of "You Are A Creator!" and "raising His kids"

Email: shirlette.powell@gmail.com
@shirlettepowell on Facebook and @_shineonsis on TikTok.

Danita Tate

Danita Tate is the Owner of Chiquita's Miracle Hands, Chiquita's Miracle Works and Chiquita's Blessed Scents and Chiquita's Blessed Transportation. Danita is a 56-year-old mother and grandmother that lives to keep her sisters Attorney Chiquita Tate and Juantonja Richmond legacies alive. She is one of seven children of a drug addicted mother, even though she was the second oldest Danita took on the role of mothering her siblings. She admits that she has done things for her family that were not within the perimeters of the law and may not be what others want her to be, but she is all that she can be and embraces her past by sharing with others today. In February of 2009 her life was forever changed by the brutal murder of her sister Attorney Chiquita Tate and in March of 2023 her sister Juantonja Richmond was brutally murdered.

As a determined, hardworking self-starter and obviously a woman who wears many hats, she could not stop and knew what she had to do to succeed in creating her sister's legacy, so she began to write her vision and made it plain. She immediately began developing the Chiquita Tate brand, with Chiquita's Blessed Hands a janitorial service. She has made many strides and developed great relationships with other companies, a rapport with her community, and now has established colleagues that she has partnered with to not only put her company on the map, but unselfishly help theirs also.

Danita is moving in the right direction and has her eye on the prize. She feels giving up is not an option and will not let anything stop her. By stepping out on faith, Danita created a line of cleaning products Chiquita's Miracle Works, a bathroom cleaner and a deodorizer that can be purchased in a 23-ounce spray bottle or by the gallon. In October of 2020.she launched Blessed Scents, a line of candles and Chiquitas Blessed Transportation.. As of March of 2021, Chiquita's Miracle Works can be purchased via Amazon. Her first book release was her memoir Life of a Survivor in 2021, and her latest Empowered by Tragedy was released on October 15, 2023. She still struggles with the murders of her sisters, but the legacy she is building keeps their memory alive.

Dr. Toscha L Dickerson

Purpose: To educate and inspire women on the importance of Self-Care
Mission: Transforming Stress into a Lifestyle of Success
www.ceosuccessmodel.com
www.dickersonmanagement.com

Dr. Toscha L. Dickerson is a mother, wife, entrepreneur, author, and advocate for all things that educate and inspire women to reach their highest potential. Dr. Dickerson has always been a servant leader by volunteering and leading community events. In 2017, she founded nonprofit organization S.T.R.E.S.S.O.U.T. which provided services to previously incarcerated women to help reduce the rate of recidivism. In addition to that, she would provide free coaching services, resume' writing, and self-care baskets. Dr. Dickerson graduated from Grambling State University with her undergraduate degree and received her Master's degree from Southern University A&M College. She later earned her Doctorate degree in Business Administration from Capella University. Her passion for education led her to becoming an Assistant Professor and opening a charter school for children Pre-K-8th grade, where she is currently the Board Vice Chairwoman.

In 2018, she decided to write her first book titled Sisterhood: Traveling the Scarlet Road to an Authentic Life. Her candid conversations opened the eyes of so many women who saw themselves in her stories and could resonate with her life. After working in corporate America for over 20 years, Dr. Dickerson felt an inkling that would not go away. She knew it was God speaking to her in a soft whisper to leave her job. She decided to resign and start a new chapter in her life.

Dr. Dickerson was no stranger to hard work, after working on her non-profit; she and her then 5-year-old daughter, Kaleigh, were accustomed to serving the community. She went fulltime in her own company Dickerson Management & Associates and begin working for herself and partnering with her daughter to bring a message to women and girls about the importance of taking care of their bodies. "Self-care is more than getting our hair and nails done, it involves our mental, emotional, physical, and spiritual well-being".

After Dr. Dickerson quit her corporate job, she never looked back and continues to speak to women all over the world advocating for their total well-being. God gave her the vision to have a retreat during Essence Festival Weekend to reach women from all over the world. The Big Easy Retreat was created from this vision. She later wrote the book titled, Finding My Way: 21 Steps to Self-Discovery as a guide to help women navigate through life from a spiritual viewpoint.

As an entrepreneur, she has coached, mentored, and assisted women and young girls in all aspects of their life to move past fear and embrace their authentic self. Dr. Dickerson is looking forward to the future and continuing her journey to inspire and educate black and brown women to change their view of wellness and the importance selfcare.

The Big Easy Retreat will be an annual event where her 11-year-old daughter will be an active participant helping alongside her mom to educate women on the importance of wellness. Dr. Dickerson is an international speaker and an active member of Delta Sigma Theta Sorority, Incorporated.

Shameka Nicole

Shameka is a published author and the founder and owner of Called to Write Publishing & Consulting. Known for her unique writing style coupled with her desire to draw others to Christ, Shameka has answered the call to assist believers alike to birth what God has placed within them to birth. She has a heart for God and longs to see others healed and delivered. It is her mission to lead others to Christ while utilizing the gifts and talents that have been entrusted to her.

Connect with Shameka today!

Email: Info@thecalledtowrite.com
Website: www.thecalledtowrite.com
Instagram: @called2write
Facebook:
www.Facebook.com/ShamekaNicole ;
www.Facebook.com/Called2Write

Ricky James Allen-Callahan

Ricky James Allen-Callahan Theological Bio Ricky James Allen-Callahan was born on August 25, 1969, to the parents of Ledoris Allen and Harrison Morris Callahan, Jr. He is a 1987 graduate of Zachary High School, Zachary LA and a graduate of ITI Technical College, Baton Rouge, LA. Ricky began operating as a seer at the age of 12 through several angelic visitations. He was baptized in October 1992 by the late Pastor Sam Marshal Johnson at St. Peter B. Church, where he taught Sunday School and led a Bible Study.

After moving to Baton Rouge, LA, Ricky became a member of Living Faith Christian Center, under the leadership of Pastor Raymond Johnson. He has a Doctor of Leadership Theology Degree from Bethany World Prayer Center and 13 weeks of Discipleship training from the program, Encountering God, from Doers of the Word Ministry. Ricky is defined by his peers as a gentle giant who is humble, yet a powerful intercessor called to raise a hedge of protection over homes, cities, and nations worldwide, while effectively ministering to people of diverse social, economic, and ethnic backgrounds. He is proficient in the gift of prophecy and operates in an apostolic gift that brings direction and encouragement to move others in their gift. He has the ability to bring the supernatural to reality to those who believe that God has a plan for their life.

Many ministries have been realized through the voice of the Holy Spirit operating in him. As an effective communicator, he is called to unite people in the Kingdom of God through love that provides purpose. He teaches and preaches the Gospel of the Kingdom according to the uncompromising Word of God. He has been invited as a guest speaker to conferences nationwide. Ricky is married and is the father of four children, and grandfather of five grandchildren. He lives in Zachary, LA. References are available upon request. To schedule a speaking engagement, Email ✉ Servingfaithful@yahoo.com

Melanie Townsend Diggs

Marketplace Servant-Leader, Melanie Townsend Diggs, was born in North Carolina, but raised in Baltimore. She received her formal education in the Baltimore City Public School System. Upon graduation from Western High School, Melanie attended Towson State University on a full scholarship from BUILD (Baltimoreans United in Leadership Development). In 1998, five-years after graduating from TSU (1993), she received the Spectrum Scholar Award from the American Library Association (ALA). She attended and completed her Master's Degree in Library and Information Science in 2001 from The Catholic University of America. In 2016, for her heroism and tenacity during the Baltimore Uprising 2015, which occurred as a result of the untimely death of a young Black male, Freddie Gray, who was under police custody, Melanie received yet another award from ALA--The Lemony Snicket Prize for Librarians Faced with Adversity. During this time, Melanie served the Library community in Baltimore, nationally, as well as internationally, by giving interviews and speaking at various State Library conferences. Due to her health care advocacy in Maryland, beginning in 2007, which stemmed from the experience of her children being covered under Medicaid, specifically, CHIP(Children's Health Insurance Program) in Maryland, she received the honor of being appointed to serve on the Board of Directors of Families USA, a national voice for health care consumers, from 2014 until April 2021. During her tenure on the Board, she served as Chair of the Self-Evaluation Committee and was also instrumental in working with Human Resources to develop a DEI statement for the Board and Staff.

Although these secular awards and degrees are noteworthy, Marketplace-Servant Leader Melanie Diggs highly regards the rewards and increase God has given her. God has always had his hand on Melanie's life. She placed her life in his hands at an early age due to the ministry of a weekly "Good News Club " at a neighbor's home. Later, she joined the New Second Missionary Baptist Church under the late Pastor, Rev. Dr. Felton Williams, Jr. Melanie "grew up in the Lord" and served in many capacities. She became a licensed Minister in 2004 and an ordained Elder in 2014 under the auspices of the United Council of Christian Community Churches of Maryland and Vicinity. She believes God has a special calling on her life "for such a time as this." She endeavors to serve the Lord with all her heart, soul, mind, and strength, to share the knowledge of His gift of salvation with non-believers, and to edify the Body of Christ. With the love of Marketplace Ministry in her mind and heart, Melanie created an Online Group devoted to the Spiritual Growth of Women called Spiritual Care For A Woman's Soul (SCFAWS) in 2015. SCFAWS has held Weekly Prayer via various technological platforms, Life-Changing Sessions on a variety of topics via Zoom, and face-to-face or virtual Bible/Book Discussions. In August 2024, Melanie will be receiving a Doctorate Degree in Humanitarianism from the Heart Bible International University(HBIU), Hartford Ct. She will also be receiving the President of the USA Lifetime Achievement Award.

Melanie is also a member of several International Ministries. She is a member of the RoyalWomen Prayer Group USA and the Administrator of the Executive Team (Jan 2023), under the leadership of Bishop Enchy Ogbuokiri, where she is affectionately known as "Pastor Lanie TD". She is slated for elevation to the Office of Apostle, under servant-leader Bishop Enchy in April 2025. She also prays bimonthly in the Global International Watchman on the Wall 24-Hour Prayer Call, under the leadership of Apostle Jacqueline Smith. Melanie is extremely grateful to God for being able to serve Him through various online ministries and platforms and to use technology for good—for fulfilling the Great Commission. She is also a Board Member of the AWLPOF(Adiel's Widows and Less-Privileged Outreach Foundation) in Abuja, Nigeria since June 2021.

In 2022, Melanie followed God's voice and sanctioned Spiritual Care For A Woman's Soul as a LLC and became the Founder and President of a 501C3 non-profit organization, Soul Of A Nation, to provide resources, programs, and activities that will empower, enrich, and inspire individuals of varying ages in the community with a holistic approach. In September 2023, under the auspices of Spiritual Care For A Woman's Soul and in partnership with AWLPOF, Melanie traveled to Abuja, Nigeria. There, She ministered to and served widows and orphans. She was able to fulfill a lifelong dream of taking a Missionary journey to Africa and to deliver spiritual and natural food and substances to God's people.She is planning her second Mission trip— traveling to Guyana, South America in late Summer 2024. Since November 2022, Soul Of A Nation has provided over 600 hot, nutritious meals in their bimonthly service to a shelter in Baltimore, MD, has given out over 200 bags of fresh produce in their Pop-Up Produce Events, bringing produce from a local farm to the urban area, and partnered with a local organization, NJahiemMinistries and Events, to serve individuals experiencing homelessness on the streets of Baltimore.

Marketplace Servant-Leader, Melanie Diggs, is very grateful for her loving and supportive family--husband, Eric; daughters, Damaris, Christiana, and Eden; and son, Christopher.

Simone O. Higginbotham

https://www.rebirthmagazinebr.com/

Simone O. Higginbotham is a 53 year old mother of one daughter, grandmother of Harper Florida-Marie, Author, Community activist, AmeriCorps Alumni, Domestic Violence Survivor, Entrepreneur, Speaker, Mentor, Network Connector and Social Cultivation Ambassador. Raised by a single mother in one of Baton Rouge's oldest African American neighborhoods, the Zion City Community. Simone is a pillar in the community and has volunteered over 3500+ hours to date with organizations across Baton Rouge.

Simone is a self-starter, very determined, hard working, and diligent. A woman who wears a hat of many colors, Simone is the Executive Director of the Scotlandville Community Development Corporation, CEO of Rebirth Magazine, The Weekend of Legends, LLC and soon to be launched Weekend Girl.com

She developed the Rebirth Brand and has made many strides and developed great relationships with other companies, a rapport with her community and now has established colleagues that she has partnered with to not only put her company on the map but unselfishly help others also. In 2015 she released her long awaited memoir Caged By Words- Something Like A Memoir about her journey during her abusive marriage.

Acknowledgements and Awards
SwagHer Magazine I'm Diva Award 2012 Featured Cover Story

Folakemi "Kemi" Stinson

Folakemi Stinson, also known as Kemi, uses her social media platforms and YouTube channel @BeautifulResolveWithKemi to empower and inspire women to move beyond their unique circumstances and challenges to operate in their God-given purpose. On her channel, she hosts a talk show where individuals from around the world can share their stories of overcoming challenges with God's help. Additionally, she regularly shares words of encouragement with her worldwide following.

Folakemi is a creative and role model known for her individuality and unshakeable faith, and who is passionate about helping others succeed in improving their lives and their professional and personal relationships.

Furthermore, Folakemi is a licensed minister, public speaker, YouTuber, podcaster, model, and life/relationship/career coach. She is also the CEO of several businesses, including Beautiful Resolve One-on-One Coaching, KMA (Kemi's Mentorship Academy), Financial Restoration Solutions, and a few faceless branded companies for in-home client care services and other for real estate. For over ten years, her mission has been to remind others that the plans God has for their life are achievable even if they feel like they have missed God-given opportunities, have been robbed of their purpose, or have been delayed from their destiny.

The companies she has founded combine her passion for coaching and mentoring others into purpose-driven success in their personal and professional lives and her heart to support, guide and empower people through the deeply personal and spiritual growth needed to walk in their full potential in Christ.

Folakemi has gained firsthand experience throughout her life with overcoming setbacks and challenges, navigating grief and loss, and overcoming trauma in many forms, some of which include being a sexual assault survivor and having experienced poverty and homelessness while on the path to becoming the woman she is today. Through these experiences, she found purpose in spreading a message of hope known as Beautiful Resolve.

She found joy, strength, and confirmation of her calling as she connected with her authenticity, found her voice, and shared her faith with her audience that God's plans and vision for their lives wouldn't fail and that pain doesn't disqualify her or anyone else from their purpose. From that place of resolve she created a worldwide community as a supportive space where others can grow spiritually, be encouraged to continue forward and overcome challenges, and reach their full potential in every aspect of their lives, all while having fun. She used vlogs, lives, and even wrote a book to share life lessons and testimonies to inspire and remind others that despite how their story has been that it can still become beautiful.

Folakemi hoped that her story could be used to encourage others to believe that with God nothing is impossible. As she stands today having overcome countless adversities to be an international master coach, a community leader, an entrepreneur, a published author, and a staple and part of a foundation of so many people's success, she wants to be most known for how she leads, loves, and serves others through Christ.

That is how her community has come to know her, and BR Proud News recognized her as one of the top life coaches in Louisiana.

Her core belief is that " with God nothing is impossible!" (Luke 1:37), and she aims to use not only her life, and her example, but to also continue to dedicate herself to providing practical guidance and support to help people receive the life and love that had for them once seemed impossible.

Bridgette Dunn

Born and raised in the small town of Silsbee, Texas, Bridgette Dunn has dedicated over 30 years of her life to serving others through her ministry.

As the owner of Bread of Life Ministries, she has made it her mission to uplift and empower those in need. Under her leadership, the organization has flourished, providing invaluable services such as mentoring, volunteering, feeding the homeless, and praying with nursing home residents.

Bridgette also takes great pride in assembling care bags for underprivileged individuals, ensuring that they feel cared for and valued. A mother of three and a proud grandmother of eight, Bridgette's family is her greatest joy and motivation. Her nurturing spirit extends beyond her own children, as she has spent many years working as a counselor, guiding individuals through their struggles and helping them find hope and healing.

With a heart full of compassion and a deep commitment to her community, Bridgette Dunn continues to inspire and touch the lives of many through her unwavering dedication to service and love.

Shontell Buffington

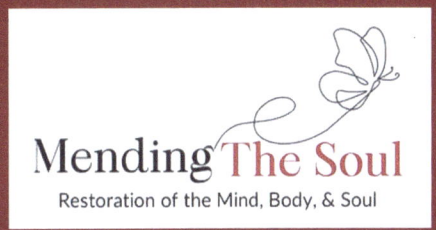

https://www.mendingthesoulrmbs.com/

Shontell Buffington, LCSW-BACS, is a seasoned social work professional with over a decade of experience in clinical practice, program development, and leadership. Armed with a Master of Social Work from Louisiana State University, she is on the cusp of achieving her Doctor of Social Work from Tulane University, set to graduate in December 2024. Shontell's work is marked by her expertise in individual and family therapy, trauma-informed care, and behavioral health assessments, all of which are central to her practice.

As the owner of Mending the Soul RMBS, Shontell has provided essential therapeutic services, including trauma therapy and DBT skills training, helping countless individuals and families navigate their challenges. Her commitment to the field extends beyond clinical practice, as she is also a passionate educator and mentor, guiding the next generation of social work professionals.

Shontell's leadership is evident in her founding of the Helping while Healing Support Group, a space dedicated to supporting those in helping professions. Her research, which includes a mixed-method study on resilience among adults with high Adverse Childhood Experiences (ACEs), further underscores her dedication to advancing the field.

Beyond her professional achievements, Shontell is a devoted mother of two daughters and a proud grandmother, affectionately known as "Gigi." She comes from a large, loving family with 11 brothers and one sister. In her personal time, she enjoys music, traveling, and has a special fondness for butterflies. Shontell is also an accomplished author, with publications including Hope Shattered, Myles Learned to Control Stinking Thinking and Stopped the Negative Self Talk, and So Can You, and Shattered Innocence - Healing Tears on Paper.

Qunita Wilson aka Lucy Lue

My life has made me the woman I'm becoming...

My name is Qunita Wilson better known to the world as Lucy Lue... I got the name from my grandmother. Everyone called her "BIG LUCY" or Mary Ann. As a kid she would always catch me wearing her hills, dancing in them. One day she made me keep them on as a punishment.

I would have to walk till my feet hurt, but I enjoyed it. Did I learn my lesson? I guess not. To this day, I dance in hills, and I walk in my heels every day. Dressing up in heels reminds me of my grandmother. I feel free in the hills; it's a part of my lifestyle. Some call it fashion, but to me it's natural. The way I walk and dress is a constant reminder of my childhood.

In 2020, I started a non-profit organization for parents with kids diagnosed with sickle cell. I named the organization, Lucy's Closet to bring awareness to the disease. I never forgot all those times I cried in that closet, praying for my son. We were constantly, in and out of Our Lady of the Lake Hospital.

Dr. Moore recommended that I participate in a Sickle Cell Awareness commercial. Our Lady of the Lake sponsored this advertisement. I was honored to be a part of this commercial, advocating and being a voice to our community. This commercial aired on national TV on April 22nd, 2022. After coming to the realization that my voice matters, it inspired me to create my own platform. I Feel honored to have a platform for my community, "Talking with Lucy Lue" Podcast. I named the Podcast "Talking with Lucy Lue", to give the people of my community a voice to be heard. My podcast profile is on Facebook, we go Live on Facebook, recording each session. I was offered to be featured in a magazine, called Pride and Egos. It describes the origin of my podcast. This platform has brought many opportunities; magazine articles, event hosting, and fashion show experiences. I have interviewed Lawyers, DJs, Models, Community Leaders, family members of lost relatives, and, of course, sickle cell Warriors.

In the year 2023, I started modeling and participating in fashion shows. As a kid, I fantasized about being a model. The feeling of walking and being recognized as a talent is vindication. When I am walking in a fashion show, I am motivated by my childhood best friend who was killed. She would tell me I could be a model when I didn't think I was pretty enough. My grandmother is another person who inspired me.

My aspiration is to host fashion shows someday. On December 8th, 2023, my fiancé Tory and I created a clothing Brand for women called "Stallions Brand." Our slogan is "It's Not on You, It's in You", meaning the beauty is within. My message to women is no matter your flaws you are perfect in the "Stallions Brand". The community loves the Brand, and we have received plenty of support. Our 2024 brand was showcased in a fashion show for the first time. I love and appreciate all the opportunities we have received.

My Motivation is my Kids, they keep me going. Both of my kids have disabilities.. one is autistic, and the other has sickle cell anemia. It has been challenging having to see my son deal with a crisis every other week. He would say, "Mom be strong for me, and if you need to cry, go to the closet." That was our way of staying positive during dark times.
Get ready for my forthcoming book sharing my testimony. And check out Stallions Brand LLC., on Instagram and Facebook

Kayla Stokes

Meet Kayla Stokes, 37-year-old Baton Rouge, La Native. I am married to the most incredible person with 5 amazing children. With a passion for our youth especially our young Queens to help guide and inspire them, I am the Director of a local Teen Nonprofit organization called I Am Kween mentoring and Outreach Program. I am owner of both KayB Fantasies LLC & Jus TrippN wit KayB.

Full time by day I work in the health insurance field. Currently in school to complete my bachelor's in business administration with a minor in management. In my spare time when I am not working or studying, I love to read and travel, hence being a travel agent lol.

I love to spend time with family and entertain, I love the outdoors and adventure. I love road trips, poetry and art. It is my dreams to someday write a book about my life and travel all over this enormous world pouring into our youth. I will make a difference someday, one queen at a time.

Favorite Quote:
Think like a queen. A queen is not afraid to fail. Failure is another steppingstone to greatness."
— Oprah Winfrey

Phonicia Palmer

https://phoniciapalmer.com/

Ecclesiastes 3:1-8 "For everything there is a season, and a time for every matter under heaven..."

Phonicia is a dynamic content creator and entrepreneur who thrives at the intersection of creativity, innovation, and business. As the founder of several businesses, she has built a reputation for crafting compelling, results-driven content that resonates with audiences across diverse industries but with a main focus on Real Estate.

Her unique blend of creative flair and entrepreneurial savvy has allowed her to consistently deliver measurable growth in her businesses.

In addition to her work as a content creator, Phonicia is also a spiritual thought leader at various events.

When she is not immersed in her work, Phonicia can be found exploring and experimenting new ways to grow within her family, reading, travel, writing, and studying the word. With a relentless drive to succeed and a genuine commitment to empowering others, Phonicia a true inspiration to aspiring content creators and entrepreneurs alike.

Ricki Davis-Robinson

Ricki Davis-Robinson, also known as The Emerging Butterfly is a mother to four daughters, a bonus mom to three and is now happily married to Chauncey Robinson. She is recognized for her creativity across the United States for all types of events and is the owner of Ricki's Creative Concepts, stationery and marketing design company.

In February 2019, Ricki faced a life-threatening battle with meningitis, remaining unconscious in the hospital for five days. Despite unexpected challenges during her healing journey, she persevered, and felt a stronger calling from God for a greater purpose in her life. Overcoming experiences of domestic violence, sextual trauma and mental abuse, she pledged to God to guide and empower others on self-worth and value.

Ricki felt a deeper purpose in her life and chose to leave her 9-to-5 job to become a full-time entrepreneur. Alongside her husband, she recently launched a new venture named ReBirth Consulting and Management Services. Ricki, has also most recently been asked and appointed to take on the role as a Marketing & Booking Assistant for Stone Tablet Music Group. Beyond her professional commitments, Ricki is a radio personality on WPFC's "The Kingdom Hour" Radio Show, airing on 1550 AM and 97.3 FM, which broadcasts on YouTube, Facebook, Apple TV, Spotify, and Roku TV since May 2022.

Ricki's transformational journey, likened to that of a butterfly, began on April 22, 2022, marking a significant shift in her life. Her resilience in overcoming obstacles and embracing lessons without regret stands out as one of her greatest strengths. Her new mantra and daily affirmation, "You are the treasure in this earthly vessel, you are above and not beneath," inspires others to embrace their authenticity and discover their life's purpose. Recently, she launched a new initiative called "Transformation Tuesday: When She Soars," scheduled once a month on the last Tuesday, focusing on six aspects: Resilience, Refresh, Renew, Revive, Reboot, and Retreat.

Connect with Ricki!
Email: rebirth.emergingbutterfly@gmail.com
Facebook: www.facebook.com/RickiDavis-Robinson
Instagram: @the_emergingbutterfly

Passion to Love and Care ministry

Prophetess Temika McCann

Prophetess Temika McCann gave her Life to the Lord at the age of 18 yrs. old and she did not look back. She was raised in a two-parent Christian home Judy. B/Tommie and Willie McCann have six brothers: Wife, Mother, Servant of the Lord, and Kingdom entrepreneur. She's known as a pusher, people person, and encourager, and she will motivate you and hold you accountable for what you say you will do. She has two amazing outreachs, Passion to Love and Care Ministry, Inc. and Touching Lives Outreach, in two different counties, Riverside and LA, where she helps her community and she helps families daily. She is an Authentic transformation Coach her Company is called One Day at A Time Life Coaching, Inc

She walks in the fruit of the Spirit according to Galatians 5:22-23. She believes people need to be becoming their Authentic self so they can be affected in the Kingdome of God. She also an Author of 7 Books' She 1# Best seller on Amazon with other Co- Author (Coach Ashley) The Chain Breaking Experience Volume 4.

She birth One Day At A Time Life Coaching, Inc had several online courses and certified as an Authentic Transformational Coach, Mental Health, Health and Wellness, Goal setting, Accountability, Motivational, Business, Leadership Coach. She hosts several of empowerment workshops and events, such as Revival's, and Conference. She loves to see women's transform into their Authentic self from the inside out rather from the outside In. she been on several Radio Station and TV G- Map1 Radio station, Cross TV, the prophetic shift ministry 1460 AM Radio Station, Daughter of the King. She was chosen out of millions of leaders and part of The National Society of Leadership and Success Conference. She Authentic, Raw, but it's ALL love.

Ro-Montee Williams

Ro-Montee Williams was elected and appointed the First National Extraordinary Lifetime Ambassador Queen in 2023 and she's the first African American National Extraordinary Ms. LOUISIANA. Ro-Montee was born in Baton Rouge, LA, on August 15, 1971, to Evangelist Purtissa Hawkins and Deacon McAuthor Bell. Her father and best friend named her Ro-Montee after an African Queen he read about while attending college. She has lived up to her name ever since.

Growing up was not easy for Ro-Montee. She has been a victim of molestation, rape, mental and physical abuse and domestic violence. Her great-grandmother, Louvenia Hawkins & grandparents, Sarah & Elijah Tyson, assisted her parents greatly in raising her up to be the successful lady she is today.

Ro-Montee's most valuable blessings are her two daughters. Her oldest daughter, Si-Arah McCray has earned 5 Queen Titles. One being, Southeastern University's Homecoming Queen. Si-Arah is a Delta, and she is one of the leaders of the Southern University Agricultural & Nutrition Department. Ro-Montee's youngest daughter Tiarah McCray was her miracle child. In June of 2006, the accidental death of Ro-Montee's baby girl, Tiarah, occurred less than two weeks before her seventh birthday. As difficult as it was, Ro-Montee began dealing with her daughter's home-going in many ways to not submit to committing suicide or having a nervous breakdown. One major way of dealing with this difficult time was making a vow to GOD to serve the people of the community for the rest of her life.

Ro-Montee has received several awards for her works in the community. Just to mention a few, in 2024 she received the 2024 Sistar's of Empowerment, Empowered Diva Award. In 2022, she received the Sister Leaders Healthcare/Medical/Dentistry/Veterinary Award. In 2021, Ro-Montee was recognized as one of Baton Rouge's Remarkable Women by FOX 44 & BR Proud. In 2018 she was voted and awarded one of Rebirth Magazine's Community Legends.

Ro-Montee has earned several college degrees. Each time she graduated with honors, one being Magna Cum Laude. In addition, Ro-Montee is certified in nine areas of healthcare. She (b/k/a Professor Ro) has taught college courses such as Anatomy & Physiology, Psychology, Phlebotomy, Ultrasound & Sociology. Ro-Montee is a called, anointed, appointed and licensed Minister. She is an Order of EasternStar, where she served as Queen of Sheba and was voted two years in a row Associate Matron. Ro-Montee is also presently the Director & Manager of one of the most highly recognized programs in healthcare & in the United States.

One of Ro-Montee's strongest gifts has always been leading songs and singing solos. So, it's no surprise to hear that she once opened up for a Shirley Ceasar concert and in 2007 and 2008 she recorded two Gospel CD's. Her brothers Eugene (Rico), Trails, and Joshua, along with her daughter Si-Arah, also participated in the recordings and shows. For two years, all the money earned from shows and CD sales was used to fund Back to School Events, which supplied over three- hundred kids with school supplies. Three years straight Ro-Montee was voted PTA President of Glen Oaks High School. She sponsored and raised money for children's uniforms, pep rallies, athletic teams, and other high school activities. Ro-Montee, along with one of her best friends, Pamela Fortner, was the first to give the Security Dads of Glen Oaks High an Appreciation & Awards Ceremony. Ro-Montee continues to serve the community by funding, hosting, and co-hosting Back to School events, children's dance contests, Easter Egg Hunts, and Christmas Toy giveaways, and she crowns over 1000 kids every year at various events. Ro-Montee is determined to make over 1000 kids happy every year. Ro-Montee has polished fingernails (not a professional) at female homeless shelters. Three to four times a year, she raises money and gathers volunteers to feed the community under the Convention Street bridge in Baton Rouge. In her spare time, Ro-Montee takes special prayer requests before hosting prayer time on Facebook. Ro-Montee is also a speaker who encourages women who have been broken due to domestic violence, the loss of a child, molestation, and rape. In 2019, Ro-Montee hosted her first annual, Ro-Montee Celebrates All Queens Event. There, she honored all women in attendance as queens while treating them to dinner, humorous entertainment, and presenting a few of Baton Rouge's most intensifying motivational speakers. Ro-Montee has surprised various police precincts with cake and sandwiches. In addition to everything else, she has purchased & delivered turkeys to the elderly the week before Thanksgiving.

Having over thirty-three years of healthcare experience along with providing love and happiness to the community, in 2016, Ro-Montee began her business as Louisiana's Clinical Specialist. She strongly verbalizes in letting the people know that her non- profit is primarily about giving back and serving the people of the community. Ro-Montee would never neglect nor turn away anyone outside of the community because GOD created all men and women equal. Ro-Montee has partnered with many organizations such as Healing Hearts Grief and Support Group, The Security Dads of Glen Oaks High and Men and Women of Empowerment, owned by her brother, Eugene Rico Williams. In 2017, Ro-Montee was the host and co-sponsor of Louisiana's Teen Summit, which was held at Glen Oaks High School.

Ro-Montee does not limit herself to helping others. Let us not forget she can also be found preparing & delivering meals to the sick and shut-in, cleaning up the community, volunteering at various schools on Career Day, greeting the Governor of Louisiana, the Mayor of Baton Rouge or the Police Chief of Baton Rouge. Ro-Montee's next move will be to work on a big project to stop child and adult bullying throughout the nation.

Although serving the people of the community will never take away the pain of losing her child, Ro-Montee admits that helping individuals who are in need is her purpose assigned by GOD. And because she is living her purpose, she is genuinely happy. Ro-Montee's biggest desire is to do the will of GOD and to prove to HIM that HE is her EVERYTHING!

Feel free to view, call or reach out to Ro-Montee for bookings or information on her Facebook page; Ro-Montee Williams or National Extraordinary Ms. Louisiana Ro-Montee Williams.

Founder / Ceo / Entrepreneur / Alkali Food Coach
Jeroderick "Dr. Jay" Allen Sr.

Herbal Pathologist Jay Allen Sr., provides a highly qualified level of herbal food consulting through his excellence and quality of knowledge. With over 10 plus years of experience in holistic functional medicine he has delivered healing services to all communities. Dr. Jay has provided great assistance in helping his clients reach their health, internal waste removal, and critical illness goals. Just to name a few he has restored biological abnormalities from pre diabetes / type 1 / and type 2, cancer, hypertension, obesity, depression, anxiety, fibroids, respiratory infections, digestive disorders, and erectile disfunction.

Dr. Jay has assisted in the restoration and rapid recovery of over 100 cases alone during the pandemic crisis. With his uniquely created compounds, he utilizes his gift in arresting the development of excess tumors by providing the biological system with over 60% of oxygen. This prominent holistoc method has enabled his clients to relinquish themselves from suppressive medications to a natural state of blood glucose and blood pressure regulation, along with Increasing the vitality of a healthier cellular growth and development.

As a gifted Herbal Pathologist, Mr. Allen values the lives of all humanity. Through honorable submission as an humble servant he gives his life to the betterment of growth and development to all mankind. As he always mentions in the words of the late great Dr. Myles Munroe (in order to be great amongst humanity you must be a slave to your gift).

CONSULTING SERVICE LINK: https://herbal-genisis-products-llc.company.site/
E-COMMERCE STORE: https://herbal-genisis-products-llc.company.site/
SPEAKING ENGAGEMENTS CALL FOR NEGOTIABLE PRICING
SOCIAL MEDIA LINKS: FB https://www.facebook.com/jay.starr.52
Instagram: https://www.instagram.com/jayallensr_

Eartha Stone

My name is Eartha Stone, I was born and raised in a small community in Livingston, Texas. My husband, Arthur Stone, and I have been married for 41 years. We currently live in Point Blank, Texas. We have three amazing daughters and 11 grandchildren.

After 34 years of service with the Texas Department of Human Resources, I retired. During my tenure with the Department of Human Services, I supervised the summer youth group employees and worked as a case manager to determine eligibility for Medicaid, Food Stamps and Temporary Assistances for Needy Families.

In addition, I also engaged in Toys for Tots, a Program lead by Child Protective Services. I coordinated appointments and issued benefit cards for recipients. I worked with co-workers to resolved frequent daily issues for clients. I spearheaded and was the founder of Gifting to Mothers during Mother's Day. I mainly targeted elderly women/widowers around about the community. This program provided gifts to the women in the county during Mother's Day with the help of donations given to me from various county officials including, State Representative Dan Ellis.

As a minister of the Gospel of Jesus Christ, I am called to disciple others. I am an entrepreneur who sales and rent properties. I am currently an active member with Safir...MetaMask and PMC

As the National Director of the Women's Counsel for Black Wall Street, I have launched a group called the Daughters of Zion, which is also a faith-based group of entrepreneurs who are investors. My professional career has afforded me the opportunity to enhance my leadership and business management skills. I am currently a member of the Black Belt African American Business Association who are connected to the Black Panthers.

Our goals and mission are to empower both men and women by providing them with knowledge, skills and resources which will enable them to create, develop and successfully manage their own businesses. We encourage entrepreneurship for clients who desire to follow their dreams and become successful business owners. We assist clients with planning and organizing fundraising events, prayer conferences and historical cultural functions.

https://blackwallstreet.org/nwc

Dr. Evonne Dunn

Dr. Evonne Dunn is the Senior Pastor of Spirit of Truth International Ministries in Baton Rouge, Louisiana. She is married to Pastor Cleve Dunn, Sr. She was born in Topeka, Kansas, grew up in Houston, Texas, and resides in Baton Rouge, Louisiana.

Dr. Dunn has been called to healing and deliverance ministry. Many lives have been changed through the teaching and preaching of the Word of God through Dr. Dunn. Her motto is "Stick to the Word of God and you can't go wrong.

Dr. Dunn has a Doctorate of Theology Degree from Christian Bible College of Baton Rouge, La., Bachelor of Science degree in Secondary Education from Southern University A&M College in Baton Rouge, La., and an Associate of Divinity from the Ministry of Love School of Ministry. She has also attended Thereupon Institute of Biblical Counseling.

Over the past 25 years, she has worked as a television producer, video editor, marketer, and graphics designer, along with her husband, Pastor Cleve Dunn, Sr. The couple has produced numerous television programs locally and internationally. She is the founder of Royal Witness Tv Network, which airs on Roku Tv, Amazon Fire, Vimeo, and other social media formats. The purpose of Royal Witness Tv Network is to provide the gospel of Jesus Christ and family-oriented content for viewers around the world. She is also the founder of Royal Witness LLC, which sells Christian products online. The focus of Royal Witness LLC is to provide Christian apparel for Christians to minister to others through their apparel. The message of Royal Witness is, as Christians, we are royal priests and are all called to witness for Jesus Christ.

Dr. Evonne Dunn has served in ministry in various capacities and has had a passion for teaching people how to apply the Word of God in their everyday lives. She taught at Christian Bible College and The Ministry of Love School of Ministry in Baton Rouge, Louisiana.

Dr. Dunn has hosted Spirit of Truth Television Broadcast, which airs on Royal Witness Tv Network, SOT Radio Broadcast, which aired on WPFC and WTQT 106.1FM, and SOT online radio station, where she has ministered the Word of God plus interviewed national gospel artists. She has appeared on An Invitation to Christ TV program and has hosted Youth Today television program.

Youth Today taught youth how to make a positive impact on their community. She is also the founder of Spirit of Truth Magazine, which featured various fivefold ministry gifts ministering the Word of God, inspirational writings about maintaining a healthy body and hair. She is also the founder of the Woman Thirst No More Women's Conference, in which many women have received their healing and deliverance. She is also the founder of the We Are One Unity Conference which, unites the Body of Christ.

Dr. Dunn is the visionary and host of Operation Pink Empowerment, which airs live on Facebook, YouTube, and Royal Witness TV Network, along with other assistant pastors and ministers from Spirit of Truth International Ministries. The purpose of Operation Pink Empowerment is for the old women are to teach the younger women according to Titus 2:4-5.

Next , Dr. Dunn currently teaches Media Arts and Digital Arts at a local high school, where she formed a media team to shoot various events at the school and community. She and her students produced a yearbook that inspires those who view it.

Lastly, Dr. Dunn has written " No Wasted Wounds" that will help those who feel like life has them on a roller coaster ride. This book will encourage the reader to turn to something bigger than themselves and find healing and redemption in the finished work of Jesus Christ.

Prophetess/Evangelists Jill Brandell

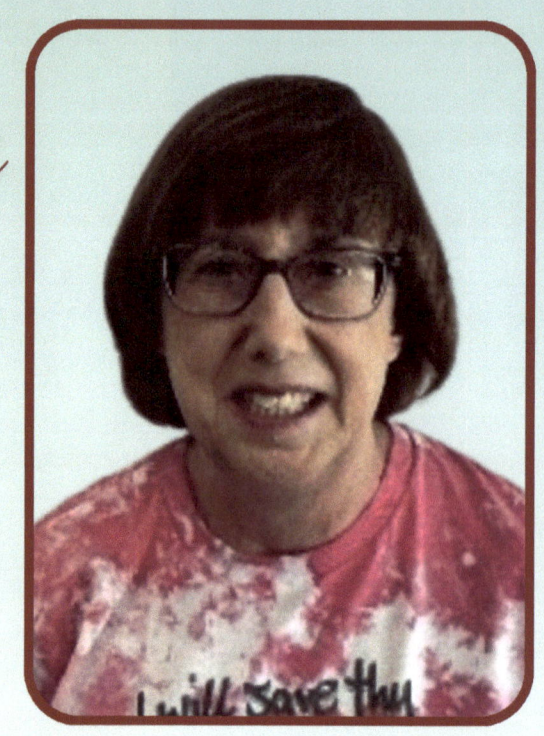

Prophetess/Evangelist Jill Brandell is a woman after God's own heart who desires to be a blessing wherever and whenever she can. She was born in Minneapolis, MN and has also lived in Michigan and Mississippi. Currently, she resides in Covington, LA, just north of New Orleans. At the age of 20, she received Jesus Christ as her Savior and Lord. Four years later, she was baptized in the Holy Spirit with the evidence of speaking in other tongues.

Prophetess/ Evangelist Brandell graduated from Benjamin Franklin High School in New Orleans, LA and completed her Bachelor of Arts Degree with Honors in Elementary Education at Michigan State University in East Lansing, MI in 1991. In 1999, she was licensed as a minister in Gretna, LA under Pastor James DeClouette of Cornerstone Full Gospel Fellowship. She was ordained as a Prophetess, Evangelist, and Teacher in 2006 under Pastor Victoria Smith of Hosanna Ministries in Gulfport, MS. While in Gulfport, MS she met and submitted herself under the leadership of her current Pastor, Apostle Patricia Magee of Code Blue Anointing Ministries, Inc. She holds ordination credentials under Apostle Magee as of April 8, 2010 as Minister Jill Brandell. On August 5, 2023 at the CBAMI Women's Conference in Baton Rouge, LA, she was set in place spontaneously as Prophetess Jill Brandell. Prohetess Brandell has traveled with her pastor and assists her in any way that she can, especially in prayer/intercession and giving. Her pastor is currently based in Baton Rouge, LA.

As a Teacher in the Body of Christ, Prophetess Brandell breaks down the Word of God so that everyone can easily understand it. In 1997, Evangelist Brandell founded God's Children in Revival Ministries, while living in New Orleans, LA. Many ministry doors have opened for her including churches, revival services, conferences, nursing homes, Christian schools, summer camps, festivals, low-income neighborhoods, and others. Yet, she most enjoys sharing the Gospel of Jesus Christ one-on-one with anyone who needs salvation. All nine Gifts of the Spirit do operate in her life, as she allows God to speak prophetically through her messages. She has even seen God heal cancer and neurological conditions that the doctors cannot explain! God still does miracles today!

Prophetess Brandell also does liturgical dance; makes banners, flags, and streamers; and does clown ministry. Her multi-faceted ministry has allowed her to assist other ministries on the Mississippi Gulf Coast, as well as in multiple cities in LA. She desires to minister to the children, youth and adults through God's Word and by the power of the Holy Spirit.

Cassandra Lang

Every woman's success should be an inspiration to another. Women with extensive experience in self-employment may be better qualified to mentor and empower the next generation of female leaders because they have already overcome the obstacles that most women in leadership roles face. Achieving financial independence and autonomy is the ultimate objective for every woman, and self-employment is the only path toward this.

Cassandra Lang, a woman with over 20 years of experience in leadership roles, has helped many women become stronger leaders through her motivational speeches and mentorship programs. She has served as an instrument of empowerment for a diverse range of individuals and groups, including community leaders, small business owners, and non-profit organization leaders. She's the founder of the Create Your World Wisdom Network Internet Radio Station. She holds a business administration degree from Remington College.

Cassandra has worked as the Marketing Director and Account Executive at WPFC 1550AM for more than 20 years, as well as the Sales Director for Clear Channel Radio Station and Gospel Truth Magazine (Kerry Douglas). She is the Producer & Host of the Cassandra Lang Show and Community Empowerment, a Producer and Writer of the "Bring Back Your Glory" live recording, and a Producer of meditative scriptures, Love Thoughts and Healing Scriptures.

In addition to being a highly experienced Executive, Motivational Speaker, and Mentor, Cassandra has empowered countless individuals through her empowering books. Her books include Create Your World: You Have The Power To Create Your World, Discover Yourself, I am A Queen and Uncover Her Innocent Eyes.

Things move swiftly in a fast-paced workplace. There's a lot going on. Therefore, you have to be prepared for new and occasionally urgent work at all times. If you know how to manage your business, you can have a great leadership career in this kind of setting. The next wave of female leaders may get a lot of empowerment from Cassandra's tips on business success.

> "Write the vision. Find a coach/mentor.
> Connect with like minded people. Be consistent."

A well chosen career role model can provide young female professionals with motivation and inspiration to progress in their careers. Given her stellar leadership career, it wouldn't be wrong to say that Cassandra Lang has unquestionably established herself as a role model for female leadership.

Index of Contributors

From the Creator - page 1

Featured Contributor, Apostle Redrick E. Jones - page 2

Create Your World Wisdom Network - page 4

Dr. Ava Brewster-Turner - page 5

Miracle Place Church, Pastor Ricky Sinclair - page 6

Carlette Garrett - page 7

Ambassador Coach Ashley Blanshaw - page 8

DNP Publishing - Page 10

Annette Chambliss - Page 11

Evangelist Paulette Davenport - page 12

Evangelist Glenda Ricks - page 13

Dr. Latasha Ramsey-Cyprian - page 14

Dr. Monique Rodgers - page 16

Elissa Boudreaux - Page 17

Kathleen Cooke - Page 18

DNP Productions - page 19

Lady Lexx - page 20

Shirlette Powell - page 21

Danita Tate - page 22

Dr. Toscha L Dickerson - page 23

Shameka Nicole - page 24

Ricky James Allen-Callahan - page 25

Melanie Townsend Diggs - page 26

Simone O. Higginbotham - page 28

Folakemi 'Kemi' Stinson - page 29

Bridgette Dunn - page 30

Shontell Buffington - page 31

Qunita Wilson aka Lucy Lue - page 32

Kayla Stokes - page 34

Phonicia Palmer - page 35

Ricki Davis-Robinson - page 36

Passion to Care and Love - page 37

Ro-Montee Williams - page 38

Herbal Genesis Products - page 40

Eartha Stone - page 41

Dr. Evonne Dunn - page 42

Prophetess Evangelists Jill Brandell - page 44

Cassandra Lang - page 45

www.ingramcontent.com/pod-product-compliance
Lightning Source LLC
Chambersburg PA
CBHW040409220526
45473CB00004B/1176